AF610614

FINISHING LINE PRESS
www.finishinglinepress.com

Looking Glass Heart

poems by

Sandra Anfang

Finishing Line Press
Georgetown, Kentucky

Looking Glass Heart

ISBN 978-1-944899-08-0 First Edition

ACKNOWLEDGMENTS

The author wishes to thank the following publishers for including her poems in their journals, contests, and recordings:

River Poets Journal, 2015, "String Theory."
When Women Waken, 2015, "What We Need" (Published as "That Which is Needed.")
Porkbelly Press, "Love Me, Love My Belly" issue, 2015, "This Is My Body."
Poetry and Jazz: A Magical Marriage, Volume I, Sher Music Company, 2015, "Deliverance."
Poets' Dinner Contest, 2015, "Thaw," Third Place, Love category.
Maggi H. Meyer Poetry Contest, 2015, "Surprise" (First place in Mini Poem category)

Editor: Christen Kincaid

Cover Art: Sandra Anfang

Author Photo: Sandra Anfang

Cover Design: Elizabeth Maines

Printed in the USA on acid-free paper.
Order online: www.finishinglinepress.com
also available on amazon.com

Author inquiries and mail orders:
Finishing Line Press
P. O. Box 1626
Georgetown, Kentucky 40324
U. S. A.

Table of Contents

"O God, I could be bounded in a nutshell
and count myself a king of infinite space,
were it not that I have bad dreams."
—Hamlet

Transit

Whenever a moth hovers, circles my head
I hear the pompous English professor
who taught "Joyce and Nabokov."
I feel his delight in describing Lepidopteran portent,
how the protagonist sees a white moth
just before he's whisked from this world.
Take notes—it *will* be on the midterm.

If this is true, I've died a thousand deaths
done the Rorschach dance with Morphos
felt Luna moths suck sweat from my skin with spiraled straws
while I laughed stoically, so as not to scatter them
treasuring the tiny opening,
the wound that paves the way for so much transit.

Explication—that western, patriarchal
need to transmogrify the symbolism
of creatures who visit the nether world
drinking light as we do sweet wine,
landing on nectar-filled slippers,
dying for a chance at the long view
as we might fit a coin into binoculars
to gaze across a famous bay,
is analysis, not understanding.

In the rainforest
I stand, stiff and giddy
while kaleidoscopes of butterflies play
on the branches of my arms.
I feel seen, chosen
welcomed as one of their own.

Together we glance down that
corridor of brilliance
we will revisit again and again
each of us drinking her own brand of ambrosia.

String Theory

I cut the fiscal cord at twenty
worked for straw to feed my heart and brain
relieved to hide among the masses.
The ribbon cutting ceremony in my mind
unleashed a heady freedom.

Today, in the hall of mirrors
I embrace my reflection
blow kisses to a chorus line of aging poets
who answer in kind
tethered to a silver frame
solar plexus to solar plexus
lip to lip along the seam.

The baby, bubble-born
is bound by the umbilicus.
Placental slip gives way
to hidden membranes
in eleven dimensions
binding us each to every world
lacing up each other's hearts.

All day I feel the push and pull
of tensing and extruded threads
hitched to my blind spot in the glass,
while mother,
hanging
by a single strand of spider silk,
more dead than alive,
bargains for severance.

Max

In the dream I hear them
clear as a loon across a Quebec lake.
My mother and her sister are huddled at the kitchen table
the call and response of their voices
rising and falling, like the flames of Shabbas candles.
Their heads are full of boys and gossip
a veneer for the old-world-ness of their father
who spoke a Yiddish-English hash
as he scattered crumbs for pigeons
flanked by cadres of brown-suited men
communing in a foreign tongue
in this, my America.

He might have been working the old Singer
culling stylish suits for his daughters from gold filigree.
A few shekels for yardage was all he needed.
The clacking of the metal foot would drown their prattle.

Battered cookie tins hold photos of Max and his girls
navigating cobblestone streets
in this urban Eden they loved so much.
He bent his head and fashioned clothes for them
while their cold mother waited,
a granite statue in the park on Fordham Road.

My mother would inherit his softness
and tender heart
along with her mother's ice
drizzling haughtiness on her plainer sister.

It's natural that I should catch a shard
from the Snow Queen's mirror.
Once lodged in the heart they are difficult to remove,
splinters in our eternal fabric
a legacy passed from parent to child
generation to generation,
a chorus of hushed tones retold like guilty secrets
in night kitchens all along the eastern seaboard.

My Mother's Clothes

Attitude was stitched on every label
forties suits with padded shoulders,
cinched waists signaling a military look.
Crimson lips and chestnut curls
piled thick atop her head
mirrored added height.

In a renegade photo
she's leaning over my pram
Medusa in stone martins.
Their accusing eyes
track her cheesecake grin.
In my scalloped bonnet
I am already bereft.

I used to count her shoeboxes;
complacent in their pastel softness,
they topped a hundred.
I tried on heels of every hue
brown alligator ones with purses to match
heads devouring the clasps.

These were the clothes of an American girl
with an immigrant father from Minsk
rescued by a knight in Coast Guard blue.
Her secrets lay deep in the fabric
embossed by the ancient serger
which never divulged a single one.

When I moved out
into my own life
she'd send me packages
clothes she'd worn and cast off like a molt.
Stuffy, tailored, not my style
I kept a few, in each one found the subtle stain
that banned it from her wardrobe.
It became a kind of game.

In her last year of circular time
I'd punctuate my vigils with treasure hunts.
Her clothes lined every closet in the house,
rose like water to fill the empty spaces.
A navy chiffon gown with sequined neckline
flapper style, caught my eye.

I crammed it in my suitcase
tasted the overripe fruit of guilt,
thought about returning it
but never found a way.
I wear it to this day, an anchor to her beauty
I can rest my full weight upon.

The Mirror

After my father died
Mom spent hours at her magic mirror.
She'd apply a dab of foundation
pinch her cheeks to make them blush,
roll the mascara brush like a teenager,
force her mouth into a grimace,
waiting for color's kiss.

I'd flown three thousand miles
to see her and be seen. I wanted
to sit on the white linen sofa
and bathe in her eyes
but she clung, magnetic, to the mirror.

I couldn't compete
with the comfort it bestowed
when she spoke to it
or the masque they co-created
pleading for validation or bright holes
in the blanket of forgetting.

Its silver cheek echoed all her pain
and by absorption,
erased her unfilled need.

It was her confidant, her mute defender
no chance of angering it
or arousing a daughter's jealousy.
No tide lapped at the shore
of her loneliness, wanting more.

The Moon Tiptoed Away

My mother used to tell a story
about when she was young
how all the up and coming virgins—
those born with silver spoons—
would bask for hours
under a full moon.

They used her for a mirror
to reflect their own beauty
traced it in her topography
because they couldn't feel the blood
beating in their veins
the pulsing of their temples
or the quickening of tendons
as they reached for a dream.

That silver spoon grew tarnished—
privilege won't polish—
nothing shone back at them
or caught their light
no matter how long they stared.

Having better things to do,
the moon tiptoed away
on silent feet.

Rewind

On my knees in the attic
I riffle through cracked albums
not sure what I'm looking for.
Sheaves of Polaroids cascade from vinyl bindings
dried glue gives up the ghost of remembrance.
Secrets lurk there, clues I need to find.
I glance behind me for the trickster
who must have set it here for me to see.

In virgin penmanship I find myself at eight
paper so thin I trace my fingers through its skin
a rhyming poem I wrote while watching snowflakes
clamor in the light outside my window.

In their fury I studied competition, the brand
we sisters knew, vying for place in parental mirrors.
The prize was proof that we existed
aberrant creatures who broke the mold of tradition.

No one remembers how the poems began
in lined-paper verses.
No purple bruise bleeds through
the glossy black and white.
Triangle corners hold them to the page
in the innocent fashion of the age.

Even at eight I knew my task,
to defile the secrecy of truth
beneath the crinolines, half-slips of youth
designed to hide our wilding souls
to block all weakness and desire
but most of all, forbid us see
the gift of our ferocity.

The Wolf is At Your Door

Come in
shut the door
busy yourself with a thousand petty tasks
to keep from passing the peephole.
The wolf is at your door.

He stalks you, leering
licks at the larded bone of your loneliness
smacks his lips.

You cower within
not daring to breathe
the lupine molecules that strain the hinges.
You bar the door.

Just to be on the safe side
you jam your old school desk under the doorknob
pile the hutch with papers
stock the house with kindling
but still you hear him wheezing
his whiskey breath rippling your welcome mat
memorizing your scent.

Would that I could cross that threshold
soles brushing stones of fear
like hot coals.

*****

The wolf and I are friends.
We have laughed together over ale
exchanged a bawdy joke in waning light.

Sometimes I ask him in for dinner
or a glass of port
watch him mark his conquests
on the night's cool slate.

Some days we sit together
knee to knee
steeped in solitude so rich
it could cream your tea.

The Wolf Comes of Age

The wolf and I would like to have you in for tea.
Please come at three.
An old man now
the wolf's grown long in the tooth.

Children no longer run when he answers the door in my old
  housecoat.
They stop to gawk, gobble the gingersnaps he bakes
see past his down-turned mouth.
They know he's harmless
a cool head that will sit with them when fear's afoot
an ear that nods and strokes its whiskers
as long as they need him to.

The wolf's no longer afraid of mirrors.
He takes the time to study himself, try on new faces
admire the pouched skin below his eyes.
He loves to comb his long gray fur
laughs at the crinkle
as he teases static from his brush.

The wolf and I were married back in two-ought-three.
Although he's lost some fire
his loyal heart maintains a steady beat.
Our twin breaths sing us off to sleep.

This Is My Body

Arising from my bed
I thrill to her constancy
sixty years show little weakness
no slack in the impetus
to climb and stride
to slash the veil of sleep
and plunge into another borning day.

Washing at the mirror
I admire her hillocks
plains, canadas
stroke the tender gooseflesh of her thighs
set it in motion, chuckle
at the swaying pendulum of fatted skin.

I seek her eyes
recall the tracks laid down across this flesh
the work of a frenzied mother
whose rage planted welts beneath her skin
scars that would never truly fade.

Standing sideways
I note the cummerbund of belly
a small satin purse
I clutch in one hand.
She must be the new neighbor
who blocks my unobstructed view
of the cliff's lean feet.

Ah well, I think, no matter now.
I grasp her cushioned elbow
steer her from the glass
and laugh as loudly as the girl
whose parents stole out of Auschwitz in the night.

Night Kayaking

Winding through the bay in blackness
paddles carve gyres in lucent water
necks arched to scan the constellations.
Greek names sit on my tongue like communion wafers
sanctify the mystery of the Dinoflagellates
teeming all around us.
The soul swells to such beauty
returns to elemental forms.
Alpha Cassiopeia is the breast,
Beta Cassiopeia, the hands
names like wands to awaken the body of the heavens
rouse the heart
lay bare the myths we were suckled on.
We watch our blades
strike the tinderbox of floating ink
serving sprays of silver sparks.
Our eyes catch fire and hold
a light both momentary and eternal.

Abandon

What if the birth trauma is only the beginning.
The narcissistic mother reaching for her hairbrush
in place of the fetid infant
smeared with blood and shit.
What if the pattern of leaving persists
through hours of crying it out
fears of spoiling the willful child
advice of experts not to coddle him.
What if her upbringing is the ghost
of the locked door, silenced mouth
busy hands of separation.
What if it follows her into adolescence
the lost child imprisoned in a cell
of her own making
the lesser of two hells
a place she can at least call her own.
What if leaving home is both
ecstasy and rupture
the youth adrift in the great world
like a lobster after molting
carapace not yet hardened against predation.
What if it follows her into every hallway
crosses each bloody threshold
into the minds and hearts of others
friends and would-be lovers
abandoned just like you.
What if you cannot stop the fixing
the lure of stand-ins for the family wound.
What if one day you threw your hands up,
and shouted "enough!"
What if you could get beyond this need to change them
to face the black hole of your heart
in the tarnished mirror alone?

Happiness Weighs More

I grew up on strudel & kreplach
pinching crust with meaty thumbs.
Grandma and I joked over kneading
grounded by laughter.
Butter cream defined our yen for sweetness
tempering the bitter in our lives.

In college I met Anorexia.
She wasn't pretty
though in the mirror she felt ethereal.
I hoped to catch a fistful of her robe and sail away.

By day I starved, loving the refusal
jaw set in concrete
spurning calorie by negative calorie.
By night my dreams were filled with calipers;
sandbags barred the doorway to my mouth.

In time, I came to know Bulimia,
her crazy sister.
She holed up in my apartment
camped out on the couch
taught me to punch down dough to stopper pain
before I gave it back
as guilt, remorse, the great re-emptying.

I ran the gamut 'til I saw the needle hover
then find rest
on a sensible scale.
Gradually, I learned to stomach love.

Deliverance

When you flew away you left me stranded
hanging onto cloud wisps.
The depth of darkness holding all those stars
like magnets to the tapestry of onyx sky
kept me breathless.

I felt my way through the heavens
a blind girl in a fairy tale
falling into black holes
genuflecting at constellations
as if they were the stations of the cross
grabbing the brass rings of planets
whipping through orbits at lightening speed.
I soon lost count.

Our story was a chalkboard fable, written on the wind.
All the usual themes sat like dinner guests, holding their
tongues:
betrayal & trust
veracity & loss
and my old pal, loyalty
who laughed himself sick in a funhouse mirror
'til he nearly wet his socks.

In the dream I touch down in a treetop teeming with monkeys,
inhabit the seamless sleep of devotion.
A child finds me
wakes me with a breath of mangoes
takes my hand
walks me down the trunk
across a footbridge
to tomorrow.

Bless you for cutting me loose,
damaged coin of the realm.
On each side a different stamp:
prison & deliverance
lover & nemesis
shipwreck & Poseidon,
hoisting your iron trident
over the nauseous waves.

No more will I travel with blinders
willing my eyes to turn away from truth.
In every drowning man I see my father
in his Coast Guard blues
the gold braid of his arms held wide
as if to call or comfort me from the other side of the ocean.
The faster I swim, the quicker he recedes
into the coral forest.

I wrap my arms around me,
hold myself like a lover.
I never let go.

What We Need

In the estuary we share binoculars
load the eye's vial,
mind's booty.

The hourglass fills from both ends—
eye into image, image into eye—
hearts conjoined
our avian thirst momentarily quenched.

Black swans float in the distance
in the February pond.
Elusive, private, hard to spot
(much like us in the early days)
they mate for life.

For sixteen years we mimicked those swans
emulated rococo mating rituals
sought the shadows
breathed rarified air
places we could dance, unseen.

What we need
is more than common vision.
If only I'd learned to lose the tyranny of being right—
and you, the worn shot glass—
we might still be wintering in the marsh.

Surprise

Each day she practices for hours
how to bend her body into origami folds
how to pack it small, tight as a walnut
turned in upon itself.
Maybe she could disappear
until the sonogram loomed
its shadow huge on the ochre wall.
The black and white image swirls into view—
a Cheshire cat, perhaps a pygmy ghost.
She can feel the miniature pulse in her belly
the manic laugh scaling her chest wall
hear the bitter nurse lip-sync *anxiety reaction*
before two hearts pounding as one
the embryo's demand
its tread inside her body
the outline of shared entwinement.

Last Rites

Those last few days I spent
at your bedside
counting the mala's beads
like a rosary—they were the same—
the zazen of sitting
at your right shoulder
your every movement a triumph
for both of us
rehearsal for sitting shiva.
The shiver passed though me
as the beads ran out
their absence a great river
falling through
an hourglass of longing.
On the bank I saw
Shiva dancing.

Thaw

Each November
the fish pond Dad had built
with shale and pride
grew an icy membrane.
I was six the first time it happened
the cataract of ice creeping along the surface
like a stealthy weasel.

My heart imploded
as I watched the bodies of beloved fish
disappear in their underground tomb.
Turning my back on the speckled one hurt most;
he was my doppelganger.

March brought the miracle of melting
watching the jaunty orange bodies
like golden leaves
begin their Haj
across the pond.

An early dragonfly abuzz with birthing
sang Hosannahs. Chickens paced nervously
tsk-tsking like overbearing nanas.
Black-Eyed Susans stood by
waiting to waltz us into summer.

You and I emerge from winter's freeze
our love preserved within the shell of pain
a white Narcissus blooming in the April rain.

Sandra Anfang is a Northern California teacher, poet, and visual artist. She is the author of four self-published poetry collections and several chapbooks. Her poems have appeared in numerous journals, including *Poetalk, San Francisco Peace and Hope, West Trestle Review, two Healdsburg Literary Guild anthologies, The Tower Journal, Unbroken Literary Journal, Silver Birch Press, Corvus Review, River Poets Journal, Clementine Poetry Journal* and *Spillway*. Sandra is a new California Poet-Teacher in the Schools and is the founder and host of the monthly poetry series, Rivertown Poets, in Petaluma, California. To write, for her, is to breathe.

www.ingramcontent.com/pod-product-compliance
Ingram Content Group UK Ltd.
Pitfield, Milton Keynes, MK11 3LW, UK
UKHW020421250726
13967UKWH00007B/2753